LE CORDON BLEU

TECHNIQUES AND RECIPES

MEAT

LE CORDON BLEU

TECHNIQUES AND RECIPES

MEAT

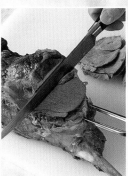

JENI WRIGHT AND ERIC TREUILLE

CASSELL

A CASSELL BOOK

This edition first published in the United Kingdom in 1998 by
Cassell plc
Wellington House
125 Strand
London WC2R 0BB

Created and produced by
CARROLL & BROWN LIMITED
20 Lonsdale Road
London NW6 6RD

Material in this book has been previously published in
Le Cordon Bleu Complete Cooking Techniques
published by Cassell at £25

British Library Catalogue-in-Publication Data
A catalogue record for this book is available from the
British Library

ISBN 0-304-35124-5

Reproduced by Colourscan, Singapore
Printed and bound in Great Britain by Jarrold Book Printing,
Thetford, Norfolk

CONTENTS

Choosing Beef & Veal

Buy your meat from a reliable source, a high turnover will help to indicate fresh stock. Look for good butchering techniques – joints should follow the contours of the muscle and bone, cuts should be neat and well trimmed with little sinew, and any bones should be smooth with no sign of splinters.

SMOOTH fine-grained flesh that is creamy white with a pale greyish-pink tinge is best. Any outer fat should be firm and white

AN EVEN marbling of fat in the meat is a good indication of high quality

OUTER LAYER of fat should be creamy white and smooth; yellow fat can indicate the meat is past its best except in grass-reared beef

LOOK FOR deep red, moist-looking meat with a generous marbling of fat throughout

BUYING BEEF AND VEAL

Though the age of the animal from which it came, and its breed and feed will be reflected in the meat, the best beef and veal will smell fresh and have clean-looking flesh that is not too bright in colour. Meat with a greenish-grey tinge and an "off" smell should be avoided.

Look for cuts that are uniform in thickness to aid even cooking, and that have a moist, freshly cut surface; avoid wet meat that is slimy to the touch. Always check the "use-by" dates. Leaner cuts last longer than fatty cuts because fat goes rancid before meat.

Buying the freshest and best quality meat is always worthwhile, but you must be prepared to pay a little more for organically-raised beef or that from particularly fine breeds noted for their succulent meat, such as Aberdeen Angus.

HANDLING BEEF AND VEAL

Remove meat from its original wrapping as soon as possible after purchase and place on a plate or in a dish to catch any blood. Loosely cover, then store in the coldest part of the refrigerator (1–5°C) away from cooked meats.

Minced meat and small cuts of veal are best eaten on the day you buy them. Joints, chops and steaks will keep for 2–3 days and large roasts up to 5 days.

Freezing beef and veal quickly reduces the chance of damage to the texture or succulence of the meat; smaller pieces freeze more successfully than large joints. For convenience, freeze cuts tightly wrapped in individual portions; use veal within 6 months and beef within 1 year. Defrost, loosely wrapped, in the refrigerator allowing 5 hours per 450 g.

BEEF & VEAL CUTS

Beef cuts are the most variable of meats and offer the cook the greatest culinary scope. Milk-fed veal is very delicate in flavour and texture and should be cooked in ways that preserve these qualities such as grilling or barbecuing. Calves that are fed both milk and straw will have darker pink flesh but this does not alter the eating quality. Choose cuts suitable for the chosen cooking method – leaner cuts benefit from quick cooking, tougher joints require long, slow cooking to tenderise them.

BEEF CUTS	WHAT TO LOOK FOR	COOKING METHODS
CHUCK OR BLADE	*Large lean joint, with some connective tissue* *Marbled with some outer fat* *Also sold boned or cubed*	Stew, braise
FILLET/TENDERLOIN	*Lean with light marbling* *No outer layer of fat*	Roast (whole), grill, pan-fry, barbecue (smaller cuts)
FORE/WING/PRIME RIB	*Lean meat with obvious layers of fat and some marbling* *Creamy white bone* *Even layer of outer fat*	Roast, braise, pot-roast (boned and rolled).
MINCED MEAT	*Pale meat indicates high fat content; darker colour means leaner mince* *Look for % fat declared on packet*	Use for pasta sauces, meat pies, burgers, stuffings
SIRLOIN	*Lean with light marbling* *Even outer layer of creamy, white fat*	Roast (with bone or boned)
STEAK	*Lean meat with light marbling* *Creamy-white bone with no splinters*	Grill, pan-fry or barbecue
TOPSIDE	*Lean with little marbling* *Separate layer of fat tied around outside*	Braise, pot-roast, roast

VEAL CUTS

BREAST	*Lean meat with light marbling* *Thin even outer layer of white fat*	Roast, pot-roast, braise, stew, roast, braise (boned and stuffed)
CUTLET	*Very light marbling, smooth, white bone* *Even outer layer of white fat*	Grill, barbecue
KNUCKLE	*High proportion of white bone – smooth, no splinters* *Pink lean flesh, some connective tissue*	Braise (osso buco), stew
LOIN	*Lean meat, bones smooth and white* *Thin uneven outer layer of white fat*	Roast (whole), pan-fry, grill, barbecue (chops)
PIE/STEWING	*Lean with some connective tissue* *Usually cubed*	Stew, casserole
SHOULDER	*Clear pink flesh with light marbling* *Visible connective tissue, white outer fat*	Roast, braise
TOPSIDE/CUSHION (ESCALOPES)	*Very lean, pale pink* *No outer fat*	Lard and braise or roast (whole), grill, pan-fry, barbecue

BEEF AND VEAL ON THE MENU

Generally more expensive than poultry, there are beef and veal classics that range from the rustic to the divine.

FRANCE – *Boeuf Bourguignon* (a slow-simmered beef stew flavoured with smoked bacon, red wine and mushrooms) creates a deliciously butter-soft meat in a rich sauce.

HUNGARY – *Goulash* (cubes of chuck steak simmered in a paprika-scented stock) is thickened with sour cream and sprinkled with additional paprika before serving.

ITALY – *Osso Buco* (veal braised in a rich vegetable, tomato and wine stock) was originally created by chefs in Milan.

JAPAN – *Teriyaki Beef* (steak with a soy sauce, sherry and sugar marinade) is stir-fried with peppers and onions.

MEXICO – *Fajitas* (steak marinated in spices and lime juice) is served in *tortillas* with avocado, sour cream and *salsa*.

UNITED STATES – *Chilli con carne* (cubed chuck steak, beef stock and red kidney beans. Modern variations may include tomatoes, peppers, black beans, fresh coriander and sour cream) may have a Spanish name, but the flavours are pure Texas.

PREPARING BEEF & VEAL FOR COOKING

Beef and veal offer a wide range of cuts from lean, tender steaks that need only brief cooking, to tougher, but flavourful cuts such as shin that benefit from slow braising. Correct and careful preparation is essential.

PREPARING JOINTS

Some joints, such as the rib shown here, have thick outer layers of fat which need trimming before cooking.

Trim the fat from the underside of the joint. Leave a thin layer on the surface to help keep the flesh moist.

PREPARING STEAKS

Steaks need to be trimmed and dressed before cooking. First cut away some of the excess fat, leaving an even layer sufficient to flavour the meat during cooking, then cut through the fat into the thin membrane at regular intervals. This prevents the steak from curling as it cooks. Sirloin steaks are illustrated here; rump steaks require the same technique.

1 Trim off the outer layer of fat with a boning knife, leaving 1 cm fat next to the meat. Discard the fat.

2 Cut through the fat at regular intervals with a chef's knife or snip with kitchen scissors.

LARDING AND BARDING

Some cuts lack natural fat, and if they are to be roasted or braised it may be necessary to add fat to keep them tender and succulent. This can be done internally by larding, or externally by barding.

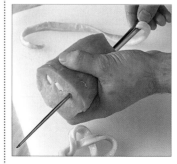

LARDING
Insert a larding needle into the meat following the grain. Thread the needle with chilled pork fat, then pull through.

SIMPLE BARDING
Wrap a thin layer of fat around the outside of the meat and tie in place with string (see opposite page).

DECORATIVE BARDING
Wrap sides of meat with sheets of fat. Place a zigzag strip of fat along the top, tucking in the ends.

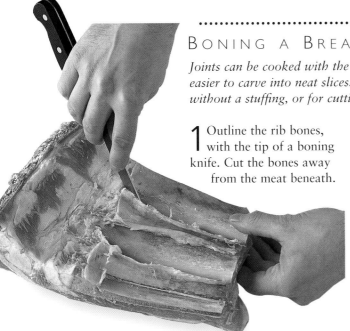

BONING A BREAST OF VEAL

Joints can be cooked with the bone in or out. Boned joints cook more evenly and are much easier to carve into neat slices. After boning, the meat is ready for rolling and tying, with or without a stuffing, or for cutting into pieces.

1 Outline the rib bones, with the tip of a boning knife. Cut the bones away from the meat beneath.

2 Cut through the cartilage and around the breast-bone. Remove the bone.

3 Remove the rib bones. Trim the breast of any cartilage, sinew or excess fat.

ROLLING, STUFFING AND TYING

Boneless joints can be tied to make neat packages for roasting or braising, or to hold barding fat in place (see opposite page) or a rolled stuffed joint together. Stuffings for joints add flavour and help lubricate the meat from inside; they also help "stretch" the meat and make it go further.

1 Place the boned breast, skin-side down, on a board. Spread the stuffing evenly over the surface.

2 Starting from the thick end, roll up the joint, smoothing it into a neat shape for tying.

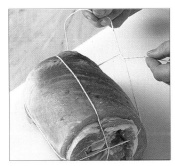

3 Wrap the string twice around the length of the roll. Tie off, but do not cut.

4 Wrap the string around one hand and tuck the end of the string over it to create a loop. Slip the loop on to the meat and tighten. Repeat along the roll. Knot the ends to secure.

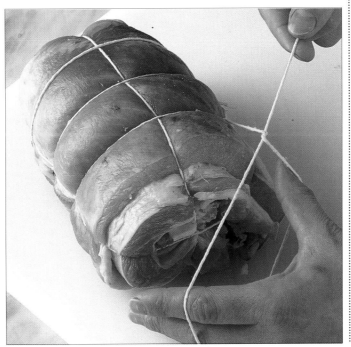

TRICK OF THE TRADE

SIMPLE TYING

Instead of the butcher's technique in steps 3 and 4 left, you can use a series of knots to tie a whole beef fillet into a neat shape for even cooking.

Wrap a length of kitchen string lengthwise around the fillet, tie it securely and trim the ends. Tie another piece of string around the centre of the fillet. Secure this piece with a double knot and trim the ends. Starting at one end, work towards the centre of the fillet, tying pieces of string at about 2 cm intervals knotting and trimming the ends as you go.

CARVING A LEG ON THE BONE

After removing the joint from the oven, lift it out of the tin and let it rest, covered loosely with foil, for 10–15 minutes. Use a fork to steady the meat, not pierce it, during carving.

CARVING A RACK
Place the rack, ribs facing down, on a cutting board. Hold the rack steady and cut between the ribs with a chef's knife, using a sawing action.

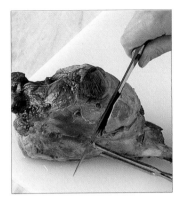

1 Insert a chef's knife into the knuckle end of the joint. Make two deep cuts, one vertical and one horizontal, to form a wedge.

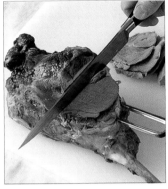

2 Carve neat slices from either side of the wedge. Turn the leg over; with the knife at a shallow angle, slice off the meat.

STUFFING AND BRAISING A SHOULDER OF LAMB

This method produces very tender, flavoursome meat for a boned shoulder and has the added bonus of a moist stuffing that makes the meat go further. After rolling the meat around the stuffing, tie it with string according to the instructions on page 20 so that it keeps a compact shape and is easy to slice.

1 Open out the meat and spread the stuffing evenly, leaving the edges bare.

2 Brown the rolled joint of lamb thoroughly over a moderate to high heat before adding the onions. This helps give a good, rich colour and flavour to the finished dish.

BRAISED LAMB WITH HERB STUFFING

2 kg shoulder of lamb
4 tbsp chopped fresh herbs
2 garlic cloves, finely chopped
1 shallot, finely chopped
100 g fresh breadcrumbs
Salt and freshly ground pepper
1 egg, lightly beaten
2 tbsp olive oil
100 g baby onions, peeled
300 ml brown stock (see page 45)
3 carrots, sliced

Bone the lamb (see page 22) and finely chop the meat trimmings. Combine the chopped meat with the herbs, garlic, shallot, breadcrumbs and seasoning, then bind with the egg. Spread the mixture over the meat, roll and tie, then season and brown in hot oil in a flameproof casserole. Add the onions and stock, cover and braise at 170°C for 1¹⁄₂–2 hours, adding the carrots for the last 30 minutes. Check the seasoning. Serves 4–6.

FINISHING TOUCHES

Use edible decorations to enhance the presentation of whole roasted joints and individual cuts and slices of beef, veal, lamb and pork. Place the decorations around joints on a serving platter or alongside the slices of meat on individual dinner plates, not on the sauce or gravy.

DRESSING UP MEAT

When serving hot meat, make sure that any accompanying decorations that are to be eaten are also served hot. Traditional garnishes and accompaniments are given here, plus a few more unusual suggestions.

- With roast pork, serve traditional apple sauce plus apple rings fried in butter and sprigs of fresh sage.
- With roast lamb, serve mint sauce or jelly, or redcurrant jelly. Fresh mint sprigs are the traditional garnish.
- Serve roast beef with mustard or horseradish, and garnish with watercress.
- Roast veal, in classic French cuisine, is served with *jus* and garnished with parsley sprigs.
- *A la bourguignonne* is a classic French presentation for beef. Sauté quartered button mushrooms and blanched pearl onions in butter until they are tender. Spoon them around beef with a red wine sauce.
- With roast veal or grilled veal chops, serve tiny vegetable fritters or rösti.
- With roast meat of any kind, toss turned potatoes in melted butter and very finely chopped parsley or mint.
- To tie bundles of cooked vegetables, use blanched leek or spring onion strips, chive stems, sliced bacon or strips of julienned citrus zest instead of red pepper strips (see right).

PIPED POTATOES
Enrich puréed potatoes with egg yolks and butter. Pipe on to baking sheet and bake at 200°C for 5 minutes.

TURNED VEGETABLES
Boil turned vegetables, such as courgette, turnip and carrot, until tender; they can also be glazed.

RICE MOULDS
Pack oiled moulds with hot boiled rice mixed with finely chopped vegetables and herbs, then unmould.

VEGETABLE BUNDLES
Use blanched thin red pepper strips to tie up small bunches of cooked French beans or asparagus tips.

BABY VEGETABLES
Leave some green stalks on peeled and blanched baby vegetables, such as carrots and turnips.

ROAST SHALLOTS
Toss unpeeled shallots in vegetable oil and roast at 200°C until the skins are crisp, 20 minutes.

CONFIT SHALLOTS
Lightly drizzle peeled shallots with goose or duck fat and cook at 120°C for 1 hour or until soft.

CRISPY LEEKS
Deep-fry the very finely shredded green part of leeks in 180°C oil until just crisp. Drain on paper towels.

ORIENTAL DECORATIONS

Present stir-fries, salads and buffet dishes with these striking vegetable decorations. They can be made in advance, but keep them in iced water until required for a crisp, fresh appearance. Use a thin, sharp knife to ensure an expert finish.

COURGETTE FIREWORKS
Make crosswise cuts in a thick ribbon of courgette, leaving one long edge intact. Roll up and stand, cut-edge up.

CARROT FLOWERS
Make four angled cuts around the sharpened tip of a carrot to form petals. Twist off flower and repeat.

CUCUMBER CROWNS
Slice a 3-mm thick strip of peel. Cut strip into 4-cm wide pieces, then cut in a zigzag to form spikes.

RADISH ROSES
Cut the tops off radishes, then cut thin criss-cross slices without cutting into the stem. Chill in iced water to open.

VEGETABLE SPIRALS
Thread a chunk of mooli or courgette on a skewer. Cut, spiralling along the length, turning vegetable as you go.

CHILLI FLOWERS
Make 5 thin cuts from the stem of a long chilli almost to the tip. Chill in iced water until the petals open out.

GUARDS ON PARADE

Typical of traditional French style, these succulent racks of lamb are served with courgette boats, stuffed baby turnips, and cherry tomatoes stuffed with duxelles *(see page 13). Keep hot with a little stock in a covered tin in the oven.*

STUFFED BABY TURNIPS
Use a mellon baller to hollow out blanched baby turnips. Pipe in creamed broccoli purée.

COURGETTE BOATS
Spoon peeled, deeseeded and chopped tomatoes into blanched hollowed-out baby courgette halves.

QUICK COOKING LAMB

The techniques of quick cooking include grilling, frying and barbecuing, where the close contact with intense heat seals the meat and retains the juices. Lean cuts of lamb such as cutlets, chops and noisettes can be cooked this way, so too can cubes of leg, shoulder and neck fillet.

GRILLING TIMES

The cooking times given are approximate and cook the lamb to medium. Turn the meat halfway through cooking. Let the lamb rest, loosely covered, for 5–10 minutes before serving.

BUTTERFLIED	20–30 mins
CHOPS	8–10 mins
CUTLETS	6 mins
KEBABS	6–8 mins
NOISETTES	10 mins

MARINATING LAMB

Lamb can be grilled or barbecued with just a light brushing of olive oil, herbs and seasonings, but a marinade adds flavour and moistens the meat. Even one hour of marinating makes a difference, but overnight marinating is best.

- Make an acid-based marinade with oil, wine vinegar, and thyme, oregano and tarragon, plus Dijon mustard.
- Add garlic, turmeric, cumin seeds, ground cloves, cardamom and cinnamon to yogurt for an Indian taste.
- Blend yogurt with paprika and a little cayenne pepper sharpened with lime juice.

COOKING CUTLETS

This simple technique from the south of France makes tender cutlets both look and taste good. Here the cutlets are cooked on the barbecue, but they can also be grilled.

1 Trim off the excess fat around the outside of the cutlets with a chef's knife.

2 Secure the loose flesh by making a slit through the fat into the flesh and inserting a rosemary sprig.

3 Place the cutlets on the oiled rack of a preheated barbecue; cook for about 3 minutes on each side.

MAKING KEBABS

Lamb is an excellent meat for making kebabs because it is lean and tender and cooks quickly. Leg of lamb can be used, so too can shoulder and neck fillet, both of which have a light marbling of fat that helps baste the meat during cooking.

1 Cut trimmed lamb into 3-cm cubes and mix with the marinade of your choice (see box, left).

2 Thread the marinated cubes on oiled skewers, leaving space in between to ensure even cooking.

3 Place kebabs on the oiled rack of a preheated barbecue and cook, turning, for 6–8 minutes. Alternatively, cook the kebabs under a hot grill, about 5 cm away from the heat, for the same length of time as before.

COOKING A BUTTERFLIED LEG OF LAMB

The beauty of this technique is that the meat can be cooked in a quarter of the time it takes to roast a whole leg of lamb. Here barbecuing is shown, but the lamb can also be grilled. For the technique of butterflying, see page 22.

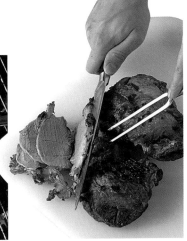

1 Rub seasonings and olive oil over the lamb. Place, meat-side down, on the oiled rack of a preheated barbecue.

2 Cook for 20–30 minutes, turning once, until the outside is charred and the meat is tender when pierced.

3 Put the lamb on a board, cover loosely with foil and let rest 10 minutes. Carve crosswise into slices.

CHARGRILLING

As an alternative to grilling and barbecuing, chargrilling is perfect for quick cooking small cuts. Chump chops are shown here; noisettes can also be chargrilled.

Brush a stovetop grill pan with olive oil and heat until very hot but not smoking. Add the chops and cook for 10–15 minutes until tender, turning once.

SAUTEING TENDER CUTS OF LAMB

Use this technique for escalopes cut from a leg of lamb as shown here, or for noisettes cut from the saddle (see page 30). Both of these are very lean and tender, perfect for quick pan-frying. Escalopes take 2–3 minutes on each side, noisettes take 4–5 minutes.

1 Add lamb to foaming oil and butter and sauté for 4–6 minutes, turning once.

PAN-FRYING IN CAUL

Pig's caul (see box, page 41) is used by professional chefs for pan-frying delicate meat such as the small nuggets of lamb shown here. The caul protects the meat and melts into it during cooking, making it moist.

Wrap about 25 g caul around each nugget of lamb. Heat oil and butter in a sauté pan until the butter is foaming. Add the lamb and pan-fry for 4–5 minutes on each side. Drain well before serving.

STOVETOP GRILL

This ridged cast-iron pan is good for cooking meat on top of the stove. Even at extremely high temperatures it is virtually non-stick, so needs only a very small amount of oil. The ridges on the pan produce seared markings on the meat similar to those achieved on a barbecue.

2 Transfer the lamb to a serving plate. Add double cream and fresh thyme to the pan juices and simmer, stirring, until reduced by one-third. Spoon over the lamb.

Noisettes d'agneau au thym, tian provençale

Boneless lamb noisettes, cut from the saddle, are succulent and tender. Here they are scented with thyme and served with individual gratins of courgettes, onions and tomatoes. These take their name from the French word tian, *for the earthenware dish in which they were traditionally baked.*

SERVES 4

1 saddle of lamb

50 ml olive oil

1 bunch of fresh thyme sprigs

Salt and freshly ground pepper

50 g unsalted butter

FOR THE JUS

1 tbsp olive oil

Lamb bones, chopped

150 g mirepoix of diced onion, carrot and celery

2 garlic cloves, crushed

1 litre veal stock

1 tbsp tomato purée

1 bouquet garni containing a lot of thyme

TO SERVE

Petits tians (see box, above right)

Fresh parsley sprigs

Bone the saddle of lamb and cut into noisettes (see box, below); reserve the bones.

Put the noisettes in a dish, pour the oil over them and add the thyme sprigs and pepper. Turn the noisettes to coat with the oil and thyme, cover and leave in a cool place to marinate overnight.

To make the jus, heat the oil in a saucepan and brown the reserved lamb bones. Add the *mirepoix* and garlic and brown with the bones, then add the stock and stir well. Add the tomato purée, mix well, and cook for 1 minute. Add the bouquet garni. Bring to the boil, skimming the surface, then lower the heat and simmer gently for 30 minutes. Strain and season.

Melt the butter in a large frying pan, then increase the heat to high. Shake excess oil from the noisettes, season to taste and add them to the pan. Pan-fry for 4 minutes, turning once, until the noisettes are richly browned on both sides but still quite pink in the centre

Arrange the noisettes on warmed plates with the petits tians. Pour jus around the noisettes and garnish with parsley sprigs.

PETITS TIANS

Sweat 300 g finely chopped onions in 50 ml olive oil. Put one-quarter in a 7.5-cm metal ring on an oiled baking sheet. Slice and blanch 200 g courgettes. Slice 150 g cherry tomatoes. Arrange a few courgette and tomato slices over the onions, alternating them in a circle; season. Remove ring and repeat to make 4 tians. Sprinkle with breadcrumbs, chopped thyme and olive oil. Bake at 180°C for 10 minutes.

Cutting Noisettes

The double loin of lamb, which is joined along the backbone of the lamb, is called the saddle. Once the saddle is boned, these two loins can be cut into 3–cm thick slices and chargrilled or fried. These slices are called noisettes *in French.*

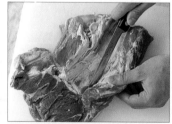

Place the saddle fat-side down, and cut off the flaps on either side of the backbone with a boning knife.

Holding the knife close to the bone, cut and scrape down both sides of the backbone to release the two slender fillets.

Cut each fillet crosswise into 6 even slices using a chef's knife. Flatten each slighlty using the side of the knife.

CHOOSING PORK

Once considered a fatty meat, pigs are now bred to produce much leaner meat.
In fact, some cuts are so lean that they require basting as they roast. Pork is sold
fresh as both large and small cuts and is also available cured and smoked.
Different curing methods produce variously flavoured bacon and ham, which can
then be smoked. Bacon that is left unsmoked is often referred to as "green".

THERE IS GENERALLY little
marbling within pork meat

THE PALE PINK flesh will be
darker in the leg and
shoulder cuts

THE MAIN LAYER of fat
encases the flesh and should
be well trimmed by the
butcher before purchase

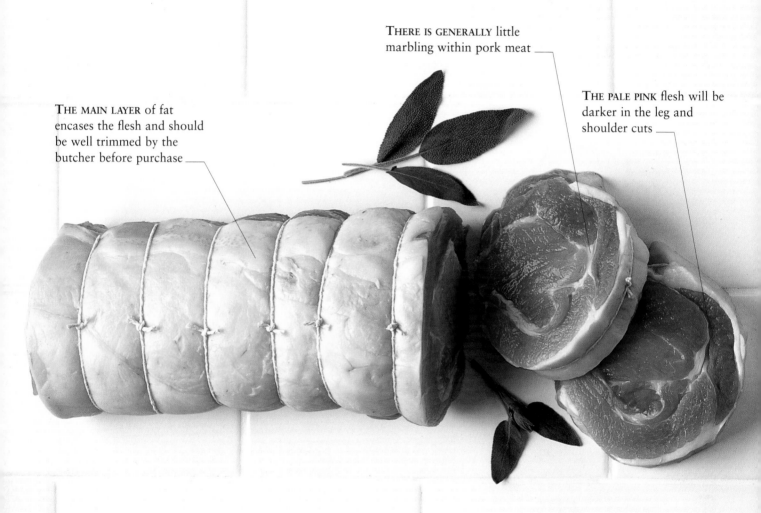

BUYING PORK

Larger roasts will often be sold with the papery outer skin – this
should feel fresh and moist and be free of hairs and elastic.
Always select pork that has smooth pink flesh that is moist but
not damp or oily looking. The fat should be firm and white.
Avoid cuts that have waxy, yellowing fat.

Bones may have a blue tinge and any cut ends should be red
and spongy – the whiter the ends the older the animal before
slaughter and as a result the meat may be less tender.

Ham is the cured hind leg of a pig, smoked or salted and
smoked. Ham is sold cooked or raw. When buying raw ham such
as Parma ham, choose pieces with creamy white fat and deep
pink flesh. Slices should look moist and lay flat, not dry and
curled at the edges.

HANDLING PORK

Because it can harbour a parasite that causes worms, pork must
be thoroughly cooked (see page 33). Store pork in its original
wrapping in the coldest part of the refrigerator (between
1–5°C), away from cooked meats. Always check the "use-by"
dates. Fresh pork will keep for 2–3 days (smaller cuts do spoil
more quickly), cooked pork 4–5 days and ham up to 10 days.

Bacon is often vacuum wrapped and marked with a use-by
date; in general, it will keep in the refrigerator for up to 3 weeks.

Bacon and ham do not freeze well – their high salt content
causes deterioration. Fresh pork, however, can be frozen, tightly
wrapped, for up to 6 months, though minced pork should be
used within 3 months. To defrost, place on a plate in the
refrigerator; allow about 5 hours per 450 g.

PORK CUTS

All pork cuts are relatively tender but no matter the cooking method, the meat must be cooked until the juices are no longer pink and they run clear. Although today cases are rare, there is a danger of contracting trichinosis from undercooked pork. Use a meat thermometer (see page 12) when cooking roasts. The joint should register an internal temperature of 80°C on the thermometer to ensure that any bacteria in the meat is killed. Some hams produce an irridescent film on the surface which can be off-putting. This is a normal reaction between the natural fats and the curing process, which is harmless and does not affect the quality of the meat.

PORK CUTS	WHAT TO LOOK FOR	COOKING METHODS
BACON	Clear, pink, moist meat An even layer of white fat	Grill, fry
BELLY	Visible layers of fat through meat Meat and fat in equal proportions Skin intact and smooth	Roast, pot-roast Grill, barbecue, stew (slices)
CHUMP CHOPS/STEAKS	Very light marbling Thin layer of creamy white fat White bones with red spongy centre	Barbecue, grill, fry, roast, stew, braise
ESCALOPE	Deep pink flesh An even, smooth texture No outer fat or skin	Grill, fry, barbecue
HAM	Sweet smelling, moist, but not wet, meat	Roast
LEG	Lean moist meat with very little visible marbling Some connective tissue Even outer layer of fat under rind which should be hairless, elastic and scored	Roast, pot-roast, braise
LEG/SHOULDER STEAKS	Some marbling visible throughout Dark pink, moist flesh No outer fat or skin	Grill, fry, barbecue, stew, braise
LOIN	Very lean with no visible marbling Clean cut bone with no splinters Thin even outer layer of fat May have skin intact	Roast, pot-roast, braise Grill, fry, barbecue, stew (chops)
MINCE	Clear pink meat with specks of fat	Pasta sauces, stuffings, meatloaf
SHOULDER (hand and spring)	Light marbling Some connective tissue Even outer layer of white fat Elastic skin	Roast, pot-roast (whole) Grill, stew (boned and cubed)
SPARE RIBS	Pink moist flesh with very light marbling Clean cut bones with no splinters	Grill, roast, barbecue
TENDERLOIN/FILLET	Leanest cut, no visible fat Moist pink flesh	Roast, grill, fry, barbecue

PORK ON THE MENU

From East to West, versatile pork pairs with a myriad of flavours to excite a multitude of cultural palates.

CHINA – *Sweet and Sour Spare Ribs* (ribs marinated in a savoury soy, hoisin, sherry, ginger and garlic sauce) is a very popular, and highly exported, dish.

CYPRUS – *Afelia* (pork stew marinated then cooked in red wine) gets its distinctive flavour from typical island spices such as cumin, coriander and cinnamon.

GERMANY – *Knackwurst* (pork sausage with cumin and garlic) is a quintessential and much loved pork snack.

GREAT BRITAIN – *Roast Pork* (pork roasted and topped with crackling) is a comforting, old-fashioned favourite, usually served with sage and onion stuffing.

UNITED STATES – *Boston Baked Beans* (salt pork with beans, molasses, tomato and mustard) was introduced by Puritan settlers in New England.

PREPARING PORK FOR COOKING

The correct preparation of pork is a very important part of a cook's repertoire, because so much of the pig is suitable for cooking and the range of pork dishes is vast. The techniques shown here include boning, stuffing and rolling a whole pork loin, cutting pockets in chops, and preparing and stuffing tenderloins.

STUFFINGS FOR A BONED LOIN

- Fresh sage leaves and whole dried apricots soaked in a little white wine.
- Diced apple, onion and fresh breadcrumbs moistened with cider vinegar.
- Snipped bacon, plump raisins and cooked rice seasoned with black pepper and chopped fresh parsley.

TRICK OF THE TRADE

TUNNEL STUFFING

This simple technique makes a pocket in a boned and rolled loin of pork. It saves having to untie and reroll the joint.

Insert the tip of a small knife into the eye of the loin and work to make a tunnel right through. Spoon stuffing into tunnel.

BONING A LOIN

Although most butchers will bone a loin of pork if asked, you can easily do the job yourself with a boning knife. Remove any skin and trim the excess fat before boning, stuffing, rolling and roasting (see page 36).

1 Holding the loin, cut between the ribs; do not cut the meat deeper than the thickness of the ribs.

2 Cut down behind the ribs using a cleaver, cleaning as much meat off the bones as possible.

3 Work the knife around and under the chine bone, lifting it away from the meat as you cut.

4 Open the loin out flat and then cut two lengthwise slits through the meat, taking care not to cut right through. Insert stuffing (see box, above left).

5 Roll up the loin, starting at one of the long sides, and tie securely with kitchen string (see page 9). The joint is now ready for cooking.

STUFFING PORK CHOPS

By making a single horizontal cut in a pork chop you can create a pocket to contain a stuffing. This adds flavour and helps make the meat go further, as well as basting the meat on the inside during cooking and making it moist. The most suitable chops for this technique are those cut from the loin. They can be pan-fried or grilled, or braised in the oven (see page 37).

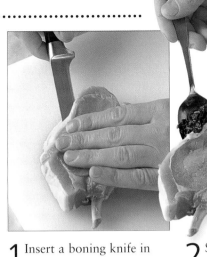

1 Insert a boning knife in the fatty side of the chop and work it horizontally to the bone to make a pocket.

2 Spoon the stuffing (see box, right) into the pocket and press the edges firmly together.

STUFFINGS FOR CHOPS

- Chopped spinach seasoned with freshly grated nutmeg or tossed with chopped Parma ham.
- Shredded rocket and snipped sun-dried tomatoes.
- Roughly chopped prunes and chestnuts with finely grated orange zest.
- Spoonfuls of fruit chutney
- Chopped roasted peppers and crushed garlic.

PREPARING A TENDERLOIN

Boneless lean tenderloin, also called pork fillet, requires very little in the way of preparation. The tendon and sinew are chewy, so they must be cut away before cooking. A whole tenderloin can be roasted or braised, with or without a stuffing (see below) or it can be cut into noisettes for grilling and pan-frying, or strips for stir-frying.

1 Carefully pull any fat and membrane away from the tenderloin. Discard the fat and membrane.

2 Cut just underneath the tendon and sinew with a boning knife, pulling it away from the flesh.

MAKING NOISETTES
Cut the tenderloin diagonally into 1–2 cm thick slices, using a chef's knife.

STUFFING TENDERLOINS

There are several ways in which pork tenderloins can be stuffed. The first shown here splits a whole tenderloin so that it can be opened out, flattened slightly, stuffed and reshaped; the second goes one step further and ties two split tenderloins together around a stuffing to make a larger, more substantial joint. Both can be roasted or braised as they are, or wrapped in streaky bacon before tying.

1 Cut the tenderloin lengthwise two-thirds of the way through with a chef's knife. Open out and pound gently to flatten.

2 Spread stuffing of your choice along the centre of the tenderloin and roll it up lengthwise to enclose the stuffing. Tie with kitchen string (see page 9).

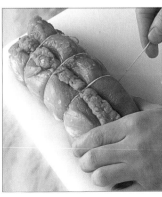

STUFFING TWO TENDERLOINS
Split and flatten two tenderloins, following step 1, left. Sandwich together around a stuffing, then tie to secure.

ROASTING & BRAISING

Using the prepared cuts of pork (see pages 34–35) for roasts and braises can yield splendid results if you follow these simple instructions and timing guidelines. Rubs, stuffings and glazes will boost the flavour of the meat.

ROASTING TIMES

Pork is usually roasted until well-done, to an internal temperature of 80°C. All times are approximate.

- ROAST at 230°C for 10 mins. Reduce to 180°C and follow times below.

- JOINTS ON THE BONE
  30 mins per 450 g plus an extra 30 mins

- BONED, ROLLED JOINTS
  35 mins per 450 g plus an extra 35 mins
  (For stuffed joints allow an extra 5–10 mins per 450 g)

CRANBERRY SAUCE

Fruits are traditionally served with pork to offset its richness. Apple sauce is the classic; this tangy cranberry sauce is more unusual.

Simmer 225 g cranberries in 300 ml water until the berries begin to burst, about 10 minutes. Remove from the heat, add 225 g sugar and 2 tbsp port and stir until the sugar dissolves. Chill and serve.

ROASTING A JOINT OF PORK

Leg, loin and shoulder of pork are all suitable cuts for roasting, either with the bone in or boned, rolled and tied, with or without stuffing. The technique is the same, but cooking times vary (see box, left). If you like crackling, buy the joint with its skin intact, score it and pat it dry, then rub with oil and salt. Do not baste it during roasting or it will not be crisp. Make deep incisions through the skin and insert slivers of peeled garlic, if you like.

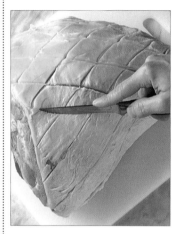

1 If the skin has been removed, as shown here on a leg of pork, score in a diamond pattern with a boning knife. Brush with a little oil and rub with salt and pepper or a dry spice mix such as cinnamon, mustard powder and brown sugar.

2 Place the joint on a rack in a roasting tin and roast until well-done (see chart, left). If there is no crackling, baste the joint with the fat from the tin every 30 minutes.

ROASTING PORK TENDERLOIN

Tying the tenderloin around a contrasting stuffing (see page 35) makes an attractive presentation when sliced. Roast the tenderloin in a roasting tin at 220°C for 30–35 minutes, turning it halfway. For a special French touch, make a jus to accompany the meat by deglazing the cooking juices with wine or port.

1 Tie the rolled tenderloin along its length. Brush with oil, season and roast (see left), basting with the juices.

2 Let rest, loosely covered with foil, for about 5 minutes. Remove string and slice on the diagonal.

ROASTING SPARERIBS

Don't confuse these ribs with meaty sparerib chops from the belly of the animal – these are best braised at 180°C for 45 minutes per 450 g. The ribs here are the Chinese finger-food ribs which need to be roasted so the meat is crisp enough to bite off the bones. If they are sold in a sheet, separate them with a cleaver or chef's knife.

1 Put the ribs in a single layer in a roasting tin, brush with your chosen glaze (see box, right). Let marinate for at least 1 hour.

2 Roast at 220°C for 20 minutes, then reduce to 200°C and roast for 40–45 minutes. Turn often to cook evenly; remove with tongs.

GLAZES FOR RIBS

Glazes flavour the ribs and help to produce a sticky coating during roasting.

- Mix clear honey, pineapple juice, oil and a little wine vinegar. For extra bite, add a spoonful of chilli sauce.
- Mix soy sauce, oil, rice wine and five-spice powder.
- Mix grain mustard and honey and thin with a little oil.

ROASTING PORK CHOPS

The best cooking method for thick pork loin chops is roasting. The technique shown here works well with plain or pocket-stuffed chops (see page 35). The apple rings add flavour and moistness to the pork and pulp down into the juices, but they are not essential.

1 Heat a little oil in a frying pan, add the chops and sear over a moderate heat.

2 Roast in a baking dish with the pan juices at 180°C for 30–40 minutes.

PORK IN MILK

2 kg boned and rolled loin of pork
2 tbsp olive oil
1.5 litres milk
5 garlic cloves, crushed
2 tbsp fresh sage leaves
Grated zest and juice of 2 lemons
Salt and freshly ground pepper

Sear the pork in the oil in a deep casserole. Add the remaining ingredients and bring to the boil. Cover and braise at 180°C for 2–2¹/₂ hours. Serve sliced, with the sauce spooned over.

BRAISING PORK IN MILK

This unusual method of cooking pork is traditional in Italy. During long gentle cooking, the milk and the fat in the pork intermingle, making the most delicious sauce and moist succulent meat. Don't be put off by the slightly curdled appearance of the sauce – this is as it should be.

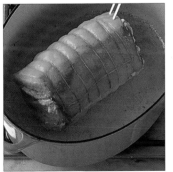

1 Sear the rolled loin in hot olive oil. Keep the heat moderate to high and turn the joint constantly to make sure the fat browns evenly on all sides. Use the fork to steady the meat, not pierce it.

2 Add the seasonings and milk, bring to the boil, cover and braise. Stir the cooking liquid and spoon it over the joint during cooking. This will amalgamate the fats and the flavours.

QUICK COOKING PORK

The simple methods of grilling and frying lend themselves to small cuts of pork, producing tender and flavourful meat in a matter of minutes. Grilling, in a ridged pan on the stovetop or under the grill, is perfect for cooking chops or pork kebabs; stir-frying in a wok over high heat is best for cooking pork strips.

STIR-FRIED PORK

450 g pork tenderloin, cut
    into thin strips
1 onion, sliced
1 garlic clove, sliced
1 red chilli, finely chopped
125 ml dark soy sauce
125 ml sesame oil
1 tbsp vegetable oil
2 peppers, sliced
2 tsp cornflour

Marinate the pork, onion, garlic and chilli with the soy sauce and sesame oil for 30 minutes. Remove the pork and vegetables and stir-fry in batches in the vegetable oil. Add the peppers and stir-fry for 3–4 minutes, then blend the cornflour with the marinade, add to the wok and stir-fry until thickened. Serves 4.

CHARGRILLING PORK CHOPS

For succulent and tasty meat, chargrilling on a stovetop grill pan is one of the best ways to cook thin or medium cut pork loin chops and it's healthier than pan-frying because it uses less fat. You can use the same technique for cooking under a conventional grill. Allow 6–8 minutes on each side, 5 cm away from the heat.

1 Snip fat and membrane at regular intervals. Brush with oil, press sage leaves into the meat and season.

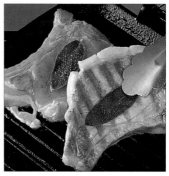

2 Heat a stovetop grill pan until hot but not smoking. Add the chops and cook for 12-16 minutes, turning once.

STIR-FRYING

Pork tenderloin, sliced on the diagonal (see page 35), can be cut into strips and stir-fried. A recipe for stir-fried pork, using the techniques shown here, is given in the box, left.

1 Before stir-frying, marinate the pork strips for at least 30 minutes at room temperature or overnight in the refrigerator. The highly flavoured ingredients of the marinade will make the meat more tasty and tender.

2 To stir-fry the pork, first heat a wok over a moderate heat until hot, then add the oil and heat until hot but not smoking. Add about one-third of the drained pork and toss it in the wok for 2–3 minutes, separating the strips with chopsticks. Repeat twice until all the pork is cooked, then return all the pork to the wok. If you follow these directions the meat will cook quickly and evenly and will not stick to the wok.

SAUSAGES, BACON & HAM

How ever you cook sausages or bacon, it is essential to use the correct techniques to enjoy them at their best. The preparation and presentation of a whole ham is a particularly useful technique when entertaining guests.

COOKING SAUSAGES

As sausages cook the meat expands; to ensure they do not burst, pierce the skins before cooking. Sausages have quite a high fat content, which helps keep them moist. To counteract their richness, they can be glazed with a sweet mixture such as mango chutney or honey.

PRICKING THE SKINS
To prevent sausages bursting, during cooking, prick all over with a cocktail stick or fork.

GRILLING
Most sausages take about 10 minutes to grill. Coil Cumberland sausages and secure with skewers.

POACHING
Add sausages to boiling water, cover and simmer for 3–5 minutes; Frankfurters only need 1–2 minutes.

USING BACON IN COOKING

Rindless streaky bacon rashers are used to line terrines and loaf tins, or rolled around a filling to be served as an hors d'oeuvre. They need to be stretched before use, to prevent shrinkage during cooking. Bacon lardons are used in French cooking as a flavouring ingredient – their strong, often salty, taste is essential in many classics such as boeuf bourguignon and coq au vin.

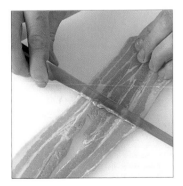

STRETCHING
Hold two rashers together and run the back of a chef's knife along their length.

ROLLING
Roll stretched rashers around filling; secure with wooden cocktail sticks.

MAKING LARDONS
Cut thick rashers lengthwise into strips. Stack the strips and cut crosswise into dice.

TYPES OF SAUSAGES

Most sausages are made of pork, although beef, veal and lamb varieties are becoming more widely available. They can be plain or seasoned with herbs and spices.

VARIETIES FOR GRILLING:
Choose French varieties such as *andouillette* and *boudin noir* or English ones like chipolatas, Cumberland and Lincolnshire.

VARIETIES FOR POACHING:
Sausages that are most suitable for poaching are the French *andouille*, *cervelat* and *boudin blanc*, and the German *Frankfurter*, *Bockwurst* and *Knackwurst*.

TYPES OF BACON

The flavour varies according to the curing ingredients (such as sugar for a sweet cure), and the wood that is used in smoking.

- Unsmoked bacon is also referred to as "green" and has a white rind. When smoked, the rind turns brown.
- Streaky bacon is from the chest of the pig; it is a fatty bacon called *lard* in French.
- *Petit sale* and *pancetta* are similar cuts from the belly of pork. The curing process makes them quite salty, with a strong smoky flavour.

4–5 kg gammon joint
100 g brown sugar
4 tbsp English mustard

Soak the gammon in cold water
overnight. Drain, weigh it and
calculate the cooking time,
allowing 30 minutes per 450 g.
Put in a pan of cold water, bring
to the boil and simmer for half
the cooking time. Drain and cool
slightly, then remove the skin.
Score the fat, warm the sugar
and mustard and spread over the
fat. Bake, covered loosely with
foil, on a rack in a roasting tin at
180°C for the remaining time,
removing the foil for the last
30 minutes. Serves about 12.

PREPARING AND PRESENTING A HAM

A boiled ham must have its skin removed before serving or it will be very difficult to carve, but the fat underneath the skin is unappealing. A recipe for glazed ham, using the simple technique for scoring and glazing shown here, is given in the box, left. This is essential for an attractive presentation if you are planning to serve the ham whole at the table.

1 Score the fat of the boiled ham attractively in a diamond pattern with the tip of a small knife. This will allow the glaze to penetrate and flavour the meat.

2 Warm the glaze until melted, then spread it evenly over the fat with a palette knife. Take time to work the glaze into the cuts so that it will seep into the meat and flavour it.

USING MINCED MEAT

Use lean meat with a light marbling of fat for best flavour and succulence. Minced meat is extremely versatile: it absorbs seasonings well and can be made into a variety of dishes from *moussaka* to meatballs. Try mincing meat yourself (see page 11) and experiment with lamb, veal and pork.

MAKING BURGERS

You can make burgers with minced meat, but this food processor method makes a chunkier burger more like an American-style chopped steak. For best results, use meat such as chuck steak that has 20 per cent fat and take care not to overwork the meat or it will be rubbery.

Add texture and flavour by
topping or accompanying burgers
with tasty extras.

• Top a cooked burger with a
slice of mozzarella or crumbled
blue cheese and grill to melt.
• Stir chopped roasted peppers
into *salsa* – spoon on to
melting cheeseburger.
• Pan-fry sliced red onions until
caramelized, adding a few sliced
mushrooms towards the end.
Season with Worcestershire
sauce and grain mustard and
spoon over burgers.

1 Put chunks of beef in a food processor fitted with the metal blade. Pulse just until roughly ground.

2 Place the chopped meat in a bowl. Add onion, garlic and seasonings of your choice. Mix until combined.

3 Shape the mixture into even-sized balls, then flatten them until they are about 4 cm thick.

MAKING DIFFERENT SHAPES

When shaping minced meat, use your hands moistened with a little water and keep the shapes fairly loose – if you make the shapes too compact the texture of the cooked meat will be dense and rubbery.

BROCHETTES
Take a small handful of minced meat (lamb is traditional) and shape it around metal skewers, pressing with your fingers.

MEATBALLS
Roll minced meat between the palms of your hands to form a ball, or roll it on a work surface if you prefer. Size can vary from 2.5–5 cm.

MAKING A MEATLOAF

For this classic American dish, use slightly fatty minced meat from cuts such as shoulder. A combination of beef, veal and pork is best for flavour and moisture, and the addition of milk-soaked breadcrumbs is important to absorb meat juices.

FREEFORM
Moisten your hands with water to prevent sticking, then form meat into a rectangular loaf shape on a lightly greased baking sheet.

MOULDED
Press meat into a lightly greased loaf-shaped dish. Level the surface with a spoon, then turn it out on to a lightly greased baking sheet.

MAKING CREPINETTES

These little French delicacies are a kind of homemade sausage – minced meat with breadcrumbs and seasonings encased in a parcel of caul (see box, right). Traditionally, pork sausagemeat is used, but you can use minced lamb, veal or poultry. Crépinettes can be pan-fried as directed here, or grilled or oven-baked for the same length of time.

Mix minced meat with finely chopped onion, breadcrumbs and seasonings. Form into patties with your hands, then place a herb sprig on top of each (this will show through the melted caul and look attractive when serving). Wrap in squares of soaked and drained caul and pan-fry in hot oil and butter for 3–4 minutes.

CAUL

This is the thin membrane, veined with fat, that encloses an animal's stomach; pig's caul is the most readily available. Called *crépine* in French, it is used to moisten and flavour food and to hold ingredients together during cooking. Depending on thickness, caul either melts completely during cooking, or it will remain and can be discarded before serving. It can be obtained from butchers, but it may have to be specially ordered. Soak for 1–2 hours in cold water before use.

MAKING STEAK TARTARE

A dish of finely chopped raw beef topped with a raw egg yolk, steak tartare is one of the great French classics. In France it is usually served with cornichons (baby gherkins), capers and Tabasco sauce, with a pot of mustard on the side. Only the freshest and finest quality fillet steak is used, chopped by hand just before serving.

Trim fillet steak, allowing 125 g per person, of all fat, membrane and sinew, then chop the meat with two knives (see page 11). Mix with finely chopped onion and fresh flat-leaf parsley and salt and pepper. Shape into rounds, place on individual plates and hollow out the centres slightly with the back of a spoon. Slide egg yolks into the hollows. Serve immediately.

SAUSAGE CASINGS AND FILLINGS

Most butchers sell casings for sausages. Beef and pig intestines provide a natural alternative to man-made casings.

- For an Italian style, mix meat with chopped sun-dried tomatoes, garlic and basil.
- Try Indian flavourings such as curry powder, chopped fresh coriander and mango chutney to moisten and bind.
- For more traditional flavourings, try mint and onion with lamb, sage and apple with pork, and horseradish or mustard with beef.

SAFETY FIRST

Offal needs careful handling, and freshness is crucial. Choose moist and shiny flesh with no dry patches; avoid offal with a greenish colour, slimy surface or strong smell. Store fresh offal in the refrigerator and use within two days. Wash all offal very thoroughly before using.

TYPES OF LIVER

- Calf's liver is very mild and tender. It is best grilled, sautéed or pan-fried.
- Lamb's liver tends to be drier and less delicate than calf's liver, but it can also be sautéed.
- Pig's liver is strong, and is good for pâtés and terrines.
- Chicken livers are mild and delicate; they are usually pan-fried and used for pâtés.

MAKING SAUSAGES

The bonus of making your own sausages is that you know exactly what goes into them. Minced pork is the classic meat, but beef, lamb and venison are equally good. Casings can be natural or man-made, and you can vary the flavourings and seasonings to taste (see box, left).

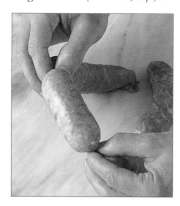

1 Soak the casings in a large bowl of cold water for 1–2 hours. This will remove any excess salt and make the casings more pliable.

2 Fill a piping bag fitted with a large plain nozzle with sausagemeat. Hook the casing over the nozzle and squeeze in the filling.

3 When the casing is full, twist sausage at intervals into links. Secure twisted ends with string. Remove string after cooking.

OFFAL

Offal are the innards and extremities of the animals we eat. Ranging from familiar liver and kidneys to more adventurous parts, all are nutritious, and with careful preparation and cooking, as delicious as any meat.

PREPARING LIVER

Chicken livers are sold whole; other livers are generally pre-sliced but can be ordered whole. When preparing a whole liver, divide the lobes and cut off any exposed ducts or connective tissue. Cut away any blood vessels, taking care not to damage the flesh. Calf's liver is being prepared here.

1 Peel off the opaque outer membrane with your fingers, holding the liver down to stop the flesh tearing.

2 Cut the liver into slices about 5 mm thick with a chef's knife, and cut away any internal ducts.

TRICK OF THE TRADE

SOAKING LIVER

Pig's liver has a strong, pronounced flavour. Soak it in milk to "sweeten" it before cooking.

Prepare the liver (see left). Fill a bowl with enough cold milk to cover it, add the liver and turn to coat. Let soak for about 1 hour.

PREPARING KIDNEYS

Beef, veal and pig's kidneys should be plump, firm, and encased in a shiny membrane. When buying kidneys encased in fat, it should be off-white (see box, right). Avoid kidneys with a strong odour.

1 Trim away any fat and connective tissue, then pull off the outer membrane with your fingers.

2 Cut the kidney in half lengthwise, slicing through the fatty core. Hold the core with your fingertips and cut it away with a boning knife.

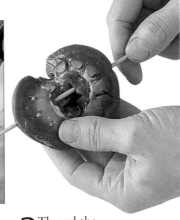

3 Thread the prepared kidney halves on to a skewer to keep them flat. They are now ready for grilling or pan-frying.

KIDNEYS AND SUET

Kidneys can be bought with or without fat (called suet). The suet should form an even layer around the flesh and be creamy white in colour. Carefully peel it away from the kidney.

Fresh suet can be bought separately and should be chilled before use. Processed suet is convenient and has less flavour.

Fresh suet is a good cooking fat, in its natural state or in rendered form – melted over low heat to remove any non-fatty particles and then chilled to separate the water and impurities.

To make a light dough for meat pies, crumble fresh suet and mix it with twice as much plain flour, then bind with milk or water.

PREPARING HEART FOR PAN-FRYING

Heart has a firm texture and rich flavour, but it can be tough if not properly handled. To prepare heart, trim away any visible fat. After removing the tubes, cut away any sinew with kitchen scissors. Rinse the heart and pat dry with paper towels before slicing.

1 Cut off the tubes from the top of the heart using a chef's knife.

2 Cut the heart in half lengthwise and then cut it into slices or cubes.

STUFFINGS FOR HEART

Ensure stuffings are full of flavour and moist enough to withstand long cooking times. Season the heart inside and out with salt and pepper before stuffing.

- Mix together sautéed chopped mushrooms, onion and bacon seasoned with fresh herbs. Wrap the heart with bacon before securing with wooden cocktail sticks or a skewer.
- Fill with an Asian-style mixture of cooked rice, dried fruits and exotic spices.
- Combine olives, tomatoes, shredded basil leaves, a little wine with a hint of garlic.
- Soak bread in milk, then fork together with chopped onion and fresh sage for a classic combination.
- Flavour minced pork or sausagemeat with a selection of Thai seasonings – ginger, lemon grass, lime juice and chilli.

STUFFING HEART

The natural cavity in a heart can be filled with a variety of stuffings. All hearts can be stuffed, but large beef hearts should be skewered or tied to retain their shape during cooking. Heart is lean so requires slow cooking, stewing or braising, to keep it moist. Each stuffed heart will serve 2, apart from beef heart, which serves 4.

1 Follow step 1 above. Cup the heart firmly in one hand and spoon stuffing into the cavity; press down firmly.

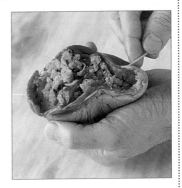

2 Thread 2–3 wooden skewers through the top edge of the heart to secure the stuffing during cooking.

PREPARING AND COOKING TONGUE

Soak tongue in several changes of cold water for 2–3 hours – this will draw out the blood from a fresh tongue, salt from a salted tongue. Put the tongue in a large pan, cover with cold water and bring to the boil. Blanch for 10 minutes, then drain and refresh under cold running water.

Poach the tongue in water to cover with flavouring vegetables, such as a *mirepoix* of onion, carrot and celery, and a bouquet garni until tender, 2–4 hours according to the type of tongue. Let cool in the liquid until tepid, then lift out and cut away bones and gristle from the root end with a sharp knife. Slit the skin lengthwise with the knife, then strip it off with your fingers.

The tongue is now ready to slice and serve hot, or to press and served cold. Espagnole sauce is a classic accompaniment to hot tongue.

PREPARING AND COOKING OXTAIL

Trim away the excess outer fat from the oxtail with a paring knife. Chop off the base of the tail with a meat cleaver and discard. Chop the tail crosswise into 8-cm pieces.

To bone oxtail, slit the tail lengthwise to expose the bone and, with a sharp knife, scrape the flesh away from the bone until it is released. Discard the bone. Roll up the oxtail, starting at the wider end. Tie with string.

Pieces of bone-in or boned oxtail are good braised slowly with strong-flavoured ingredients, such as beef stock, red wine, bouquet garni and garlic. Cook for at least 2 hours.

SWEETBREADS

Sweetbreads are the thymus glands of young lambs and calves. They are highly perishable and should be soaked and cooked on the day of purchase. Once prepared as shown, they can be coated in egg and breadcrumbs and fried; in classic French cuisine, they are served with sauce poulette.

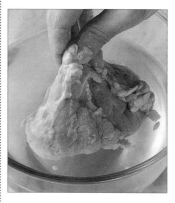

1 Soak for 2 hours in several changes of cold water. Rinse, put in a pan and cover with cold water. Bring to the boil and blanch 3 minutes.

2 Drain and refresh under cold running water, then remove outer skin and any pieces of membrane.

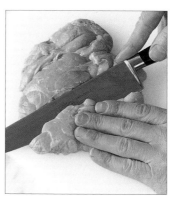

3 Place sweetbreads between two plates, put a weight on top and chill for 2 hours until firm.

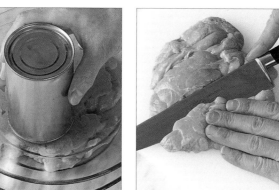

4 Slice the sweetbreads at an angle using a sharp knife. The sweetbreads are now ready for cooking.

TRIPE

The muscular lining of an ox's stomach, ivory-coloured tripe is usually sold "dressed", that is cleaned, soaked and scalded, but further blanching is required before cooking to sweeten its smell. It is usually stewed, either with milk and onions, or in an Espagnole sauce, with sliced carrots added at the end.

PIG'S TROTTERS

These are usually braised, or served cold in a vinaigrette. Before this, first scrape away the hairs between the toes, halve or bone them as shown here, then poach in stock for about 1½ hours.

HALVING
Cut lengthwise right through the middle of the trotter, between the bones.

BONING
Cut through the skin of the trotter down to the bones, then lift and scrape the flesh away from the bones until it is released.

Rinse the whole sheet of tripe thoroughly in cold water to remove any traces of dirt. Drain in a colander, pat dry with a tea towel, then cut into strips or squares with a chef's knife. Place the tripe in a pan with a bay leaf, an onion stuck with cloves, and cold water to cover. Bring to the boil, then drain. The tripe is now ready for cooking.

BASIC STOCKS

Stock, the strained liquid that results from cooking poultry, meat or fish with vegetables and seasonings in water, forms the basis of many soups, sauces and stews. Homemade stocks produce a finer, more aromatic and less salty flavour than shop-bought cubes, granules and canned broths. They also freeze well, so you can always have them to hand.

CHICKEN STOCK

Pale and golden in colour, this classic can be made from raw chicken bones and carcass or the bones and scraps of a cooked chicken. Blanching the bones first is a chef's technique to remove excess fat; an alternative method is also given.

1 Add bones to vegetables in pan, cover with water and bring to the boil. During simmering, skim often.

2 Ladle into a fine sieve set over a bowl. Press the solids with the ladle to extract all of the liquid.

REMOVING FAT
Refrigerate stock overnight, then lift off any surface fat with a slotted spoon.

BROWN STOCK

This meaty stock, which can be made with beef or veal bones, has a good, strong colour and flavour because the bones are roasted first. Roasting caramelizes the outside of the bones and so adds colour to the stock; it also renders the excess fat. For a white stock, omit roasting.

1 Add vegetables to bones halfway through roasting time and stir to mix.

2 Skim stock as often as possible during simmering, to remove fat and scum.

3 Ladle into a fine sieve set over a bowl. Press the solids with the ladle to extract all of the liquid.

CHICKEN STOCK

About 750 g chicken bones and carcass
About 150 g mixed onion, celery and carrot, roughly chopped
1 clove
1 bouquet garni
2 garlic cloves, chopped (optional)
6 peppercorns
1.5 litres water

Blanch the bones and carcass, drain and rinse. Place in a pan with the remaining ingredients and bring to the boil. Simmer for 2–3 hours, skimming often. Strain the stock and let cool, then refrigerate for up to 3 days. Makes about 1.5 litres.

BROWN STOCK

1.5 kg beef or veal bones
1 onion, unpeeled and quartered
2 carrots, 1 leek and 1 celery stick, chopped
3 litres water
2 tbsp tomato purée
1 bouquet garni
6 peppercorns

Roast meat bones at 230°C for 40 minutes, adding vegetables halfway. Deglaze with a little water. Transfer to a pan, add remaining ingredients and simmer for 3–4 hours, skimming often. Strain and let cool. Refrigerate up to 3 days. Makes about 3 litres.

MEASUREMENT CHARTS

Accurate measurements are crucial to the success of any dish. The following charts give quick and easy reference for gauging oven temperatures and converting metric and imperial units for ingredients and equipment.

OVEN TEMPERATURES

CELSIUS	FAHRENHEIT	GAS	DESCRIPTION
110°C	225°F	¼	Cool
120°C	250°F	½	Cool
140°C	275°F	1	Very low
150°C	300°F	2	Very low
160°C	325°F	3	Low
170°C	325°F	3	Moderate
180°C	350°F	4	Moderate
190°C	375°F	5	Moderately hot
200°C	400°F	6	Hot
220°C	425°F	7	Hot
230°C	450°F	8	Very hot

US CUPS

CUPS	METRIC
¼ cup	60 ml
⅓ cup	70 ml
½ cup	125 ml
⅔ cup	150 ml
¾ cup	175 ml
1 cup	250 ml
1½ cups	375 ml
2 cups	500 ml
3 cups	750 ml
4 cups	1 litre
6 cups	1.5 litres

SPOONS

METRIC	IMPERIAL
1.25 ml	¼ tsp
2.5 ml	½ tsp
5 ml	1 tsp
10 ml	2 tsp
15 ml	3 tsp/1 tbsp
30 ml	2 tbsp
45 ml	3 tbsp
60 ml	4 tbsp
75 ml	5 tbsp
90 ml	6 tbsp

VOLUME

METRIC	IMPERIAL	METRIC	IMPERIAL	METRIC	IMPERIAL
25 ml	1 fl oz	300 ml	10 fl oz/½ pint	1 litre	1¾ pints
50 ml	2 fl oz	350 ml	12 fl oz	1.2 litres	2 pints
75 ml	2½ fl oz	400 ml	14 fl oz	1.3 litres	2¼ pints
100 ml	3½ fl oz	425 ml	15 fl oz/¾ pint	1.4 litres	2½ pints
125 ml	4 fl oz	450 ml	16 fl oz	1.5 litres	2¾ pints
150 ml	5 fl oz/¼ pint	500 ml	18 fl oz	1.7 litres	3 pints
175 ml	6 fl oz	568 ml	20 fl oz/1 pint	2 litres	3½ pints
200 ml	7 fl oz/⅓ pint	600 ml	1 pint milk	2.5 litres	4½ pints
225 ml	8 fl oz	700 ml	1¼ pints	2.8 litres	5 pints
250 ml	9 fl oz	850 ml	1½ pints	3 litres	5¼ pints

WEIGHT

Metric	Imperial	Metric	Imperial
5 g	⅛ oz	325 g	11½ oz
10 g	¼ oz	350 g	12 oz
15 g	½ oz	375 g	13 oz
20 g	¾ oz	400 g	14 oz
25 g	1 oz	425 g	15 oz
35 g	1¼ oz	450 g	1 lb
40 g	1½ oz	500 g	1 lb 2 oz
50 g	1¾ oz	550 g	1 lb 4 oz
55 g	2 oz	600 g	1 lb 5 oz
60 g	2¼ oz	650 g	1 lb 7 oz
70 g	2½ oz	700 g	1 lb 9 oz
75 g	2¾ oz	750 g	1 lb 10 oz
85 g	3 oz	800 g	1 lb 12 oz
90 g	3¼ oz	850 g	1 lb 14 oz
100 g	3½ oz	900 g	2 lb
115 g	4 oz	950 g	2 lb 2 oz
125 g	4½ oz	1 kg	2 lb 4 oz
140 g	5 oz	1.25 kg	2 lb 12 oz
150 g	5½ oz	1.3 kg	3 lb
175 g	6 oz	1.5 kg	3 lb 5 oz
200 g	7 oz	1.6 kg	3 lb 8 oz
225 g	8 oz	1.8 kg	4 lb
250 g	9 oz	2 kg	4 lb 8 oz
275 g	9¾ oz	2.25 kg	5 lb
280 g	10 oz	2.5 kg	5 lb 8 oz
300 g	10½ oz	2.7 kg	6 lb
315 g	11 oz	3 kg	6 lb 8 oz

LINEAR MEASUREMENTS

Metric	Imperial	Metric	Imperial
2 mm	¹⁄₁₆ in	17 cm	6½ in
3 mm	⅛ in	18 cm	7 in
5 mm	¼ in	19 cm	7½ in
8 mm	⅜ in	20 cm	8 in
10 mm/1 cm	½ in	22 cm	8½ in
1.5 cm	⅝ in	23 cm	9 in
2 cm	¾ in	24 cm	9½ in
2.5 cm	1 in	25 cm	10 in
3 cm	1¼ in	26 cm	10½ in
4 cm	1½ in	27 cm	10¾ in
4.5 cm	1¾ in	28 cm	11 in
5 cm	2 in	29 cm	11½ in
5.5 cm	2¼ in	30 cm	12 in
6 cm	2½ in	31 cm	12½ in
7 cm	2¾ in	33 cm	13 in
7.5 cm	3 in	34 cm	13½ in
8 cm	3¼ in	35 cm	14 in
9 cm	3½ in	37 cm	14½ in
9.5 cm	3¾ in	38 cm	15 in
10 cm	4 in	39 cm	15½ in
11 cm	4¼ in	40 cm	16 in
12 cm	4½ in	42 cm	16½ in
12.5 cm	4¾ in	43 cm	17 in
13 cm	5 in	44 cm	17½ in
14 cm	5½ in	46 cm	18 in
15 cm	6 in	48 cm	19 in
16 cm	6¼ in	50 cm	20 in

INDEX